Miracle of the Holy Qur'ān

By
Shaykh Mufti Saiful Islām

JKN Publications

First Published in December 2018

ISBN: 978-1-909114-38-8

British Library Cataloguing in Publication Data
A catalogue record for this book is available from the British Library.

Publisher's Note:

Every care and attention has been put into the production of this book. If how-ever you find any errors, they are our own, for which we seek Allāh's ﷻ for-giveness and reader's pardon.

Published by:

JKN Publications
118 Manningham Lane
Bradford
West Yorkshire
BD8 7JF
United Kingdom

t: +44 (0) 1274 308 456 | w: www.jkn.org.uk | e: info@jkn.org.uk

Book Title: Miracle of the Holy Qur'ān

Author: Shaykh Mufti Saiful Islām

Printed by Mega Printing in Turkey

"In the Name of Allāh, the Most Beneficent,
the Most Merciful"

Content

Introduction

All Praise is due to Allāh ﷻ, the Lord of the souls and the Master of the Day of Judgement. Peace and blessings be upon His beloved Messenger ﷺ, his blessed family and chosen Companions ﵁.

Amongst the signs of Qiyāmah is the disappearance of sacred knowledge. The Holy Prophet ﷺ said, "You will never be misguided if you hold on to two things; firstly, the Book of Allāh ﷻ (The Holy Qur'ān) and secondly the Sunnah. Today, we are severely lacking in Dīni knowledge and have deprived ourselves from this blessing. The scholars of Islām are trying to wake us all up, however, we are busy dreaming of the present world and have forgotten our real destination.

My beloved Shaykh has started a great task; the Tafsīr of the Holy Qur'ān in the local Jāmi Masjid. This book is a transcription of 'Miracle of the Holy Qur'ān.' The contents of this speech was one of two sessions which took place on the 7th of April 2001. The title for the second session was 'The Revelation of the Holy Qur'ān,' which took place on the 14th of April 2001 in which the different types of revelation was explained, the stages of revelation and the methods of preserving the Holy Qur'ān.

We are fortunate to have Tafsīr sessions which are held regularly by Mufti Sāhib in JKN Institute, where a large gathering of people attend. The brothers and sisters who unfortunately are not able to benefit from this in person, now have the chance to read the speeches in a book form.

Maulāna Abū Bakr
Ramadhān 1423/November 2002

Purpose of Creation

Allāh ﷻ has sent mankind for a purpose, for a task, for a duty. What is that purpose? What is that task which mankind has to fulfill? Allāh ﷻ mentions in the Holy Qur'ān:

وَمَا خَلَقْتُ الْجِنَّ وَ الْاِنْسَ اِلَّا لِيَعْبُدُوْنِ

"I have not created the Jinns and mankind except that they may worship Me." (51:56)

Thus man's task is that he fulfills this obligation sent down to him from Allāh ﷻ. Allāh ﷻ has given man the intellect with which he can differentiate between truth and falsehood, between right and wrong.

Man – The Best of Creation

He has made man the best of all creation. Allāh ﷻ speaks about the status of man:

لَقَدْ خَلَقْنَا الْاِنْسَانَ فِیْ اَحْسَنِ تَقْوِیْمٍ

"Indeed, We have created man in the best of structure, in the best of form." (95:4)

وَلَقَدْ كَرَّمْنَا بَنِیْ اٰدَمَ وَ حَمَلْنٰهُمْ فِی الْبَرِّ وَ الْبَحْرِ وَ رَزَقْنٰهُمْ مِّنَ الطَّیِّبَاتِ وَ فَضَّلْنٰهُمْ عَلٰی كَثِیْرٍ مِّمَّنْ خَلَقْنَا تَفْضِیْلاً

"And indeed We have honoured the children of Ādam , and We have carried them on land and sea and have provided them with

7

At-Tayyibāt (lawful good things), and have preferred them above many of those whom We have created with a marked preference." (17:70)

Once a woman came crying uncontrollably to the honourable Imām Abū Hanīfah ☙, remarking, "Today my husband has said that if I am not more beautiful than the moon then he will separate from me and he will divorce me. I have gone to many scholars with this complex Mas'alah but each one has replied that Talāq (divorce) has occurred. I have come to you as a last resort. Please help me in my plight." Imām Sāhib ☙ replied with great ease and conviction, "Go home and stay with your husband. Verily Talāq has not occurred. Allāh ﷻ mentions:

لَقَدْ خَلَقْنَا الْاِنْسَانَ فِيْ اَحْسَنِ تَقْوِيْمٍ

"Indeed We have created man in the best of structure, in the best of form." Without a doubt, you are more beautiful than the moon." (Subhān-Allāh)

The Mission of the Holy Prophet ﷺ

In order to guide mankind, Allāh ﷻ has sent many Prophets and Messengers to this world. Each and every Prophet came with the same message:

اُعْبُدُوا اللّٰهَ مَا لَكُمْ مِّنْ اِلٰهٍ غَيْرُهُ

"Worship Allāh, there is no god besides Him." (11:61)

8

The first man and also the first prophet was Ādam ﷺ and from him a series of Prophets followed until our last and most exalted Prophet, our beloved Messenger, the Holy Prophet Muhammad ﷺ.

Status of the Holy Prophet ﷺ

Our Holy Prophet ﷺ is no ordinary Prophet. His status is second only to Allāh ﷻ. Regarding whom Allāh ﷻ speaks:

وَمَا اَرْسَلْنٰكَ اِلَّا رَحْمَةً لِّلْعَالَمِيْنَ

"We have not sent you but as a mercy for the universe." (21:107)

He is a mercy for all men, women, children, Muslims and non-Muslims alike. He further states in praising him:

وَاِنَّكَ لَعَلٰى خُلُقٍ عَظِيْمٍ

"And verily you (O Muhammad ﷺ) are on an exalted standard of character." (68:4)

The Holy Prophet ﷺ possessed such a high and lofty character that no other human can equal it let alone surpass it! Regarding him Sayyidunā Ibrāhīm ﷺ made Du'ā and supplication:

رَبَّنَا وَابْعَثْ فِيْهِمْ رَسُوْلًا مِّنْهُمْ يَتْلُوْا عَلَيْهِمْ اٰيٰتِكَ وَيُعَلِّمُهُمُ الْكِتَابَ وَالْحِكْمَةَ وَيُزَكِّيْهِمْ اِنَّكَ اَنْتَ الْعَزِيْزُ الْحَكِيْمُ

"Our Lord! Send amongst them a Messenger of their own, who shall recite unto them Your verses and teach them the Book and Wisdom and sanctify (purify) them. Verily You are the Almighty,

the All Wise." (2:129)

Regarding him Sayyidunā Īsā ﷺ informed his companions:

وَمُبَشِّرًا بِرَسُوۡلٍ يَّاۡتِیۡ مِنۡۢ بَعۡدِی اسۡمُهٗۤ اَحۡمَدُ

"And giving glad tidings of a Messenger to come after me, whose name shall be Ahmad." (61:06)

Miracles of the Prophets ﷺ

Allāh ﷻ did not only send Prophets ﷺ but also sent Divine Books containing instructions on how to live a life of obedience and submission to Him (Allāh ﷻ). To many Prophets ﷺ He gave miracles. The purpose of giving the miracles was to help the Prophets convey their divine message easily and to convince the people that whatever they have brought to them is from Allāh ﷻ.

1. Da'wah of Sayyidunā Nūh ﷺ

Conveying and propagating the Dīn is not an easy task. Sayyidunā Nūh ﷺ called his people towards the Dīn for 950 years. The Holy Qur'ān says:

قَالَ يٰقَوۡمِ اِنِّیۡ لَكُمۡ نَذِيۡرٌ مُّبِيۡنٌ اَنِ اعۡبُدُوا اللّٰهَ وَاتَّقُوۡهُ وَاَطِيۡعُوۡنِ

"He (Nūh ﷺ) said: "O' my people, verily I am a plain warner to you. That you should worship Allāh (alone), be dutiful to Him and obey me." (71:2-3)

قَالَ رَبِّ اِنِّیۡ دَعَوۡتُ قَوۡمِیۡ لَيۡلًا وَّ نَهَارًا

"O' my Lord! Verily I have called my people night and day (i.e. secretly and openly to accept the doctrine of Islamic monotheism)." (71:5)

ثُمَّ اِنِّیۤ اَعْلَنْتُ لَهُمْ وَ اَسْرَرْتُ لَهُمْ اِسْرَارًا

"Then verily, I proclaimed to them in public, and I have appealed to them in private." (71:9)

However, what does the Holy Qur'ān say?

وَمَاۤ اٰمَنَ مَعَهٗۤ اِلَّا قَلِیْلٌ

"And none believed with him, except a few." (11:40)

The Mufassirūn (commentators of the Holy Qur'ān) say approximately 80 people accepted Imān. For this reason (to help the Prophets ﷺ convey the message easily), Allāh ﷻ gave many Prophets ﷺ miracles. Different Prophets ﷺ received different miracles.

2. Miracle of Sayyidunā Sālih ﷺ

When the clan (tribe) of Sayyidunā Sālih ﷺ refused to accept him as a Prophet and demanded a sign and a miracle from Allāh ﷻ to prove his authenticity, he prayed to Allāh ﷻ. Thus, Allāh ﷻ created a she-camel from the rocks.

3. Miracle of Sayyidunā Ibrāhīm ﷺ

When Sayyidunā Ibrāhīm 🕮 broke the idols, he was thrown into the fire by king Namrūd. Allāh 🕮 says in the Holy Qur'ān:

يُنَارُ كُوْنِيْ بَرْدًا وَ سَلَامًا عَلٰى اِبْرٰهِيْمَ

"O fire, be cool and safe for Ibrāhīm." (21:69)

The special property of fire is to burn. However history testifies that not even one hair of his body was burnt.

4. Miracles of Sayyidunā Dāwūd 🕮

Sayyidunā Dāwūd 🕮 was given the Zabūr (Psalms). Allāh 🕮 gave him the gift of a beautiful and melodious voice. When he recited the Zabūr, the mountains, birds and trees glorified the praises of Allāh 🕮 with him.

اِنَّا سَخَّرْنَا الْجِبَالَ مَعَهٗ يُسَبِّحْنَ بِالْعَشِيِّ وَ الْاِشْرَاقِ

"Verily We made the mountains glorify Our praises with him in the morning and evening." (38:18)

وَ الطَّيْرَ مَحْشُوْرَةً كُلٌّ لَّهٗ اَوَّابٌ

"And the birds assembled, all obedient to him (they came and glorified Allāh's praises along with him)." (38:19)

وَ اَلَنَّا لَهُ الْحَدِيْدَ

"And We made the iron soft for him." (34:10)

He could mold iron like we can mold wax.

5. Miracles of Sayyidunā Sulaimān ﷺ

Sayyidunā Dāwūd's ﷺ son, Sayyidunā Sulaimān ﷺ was given many miracles. He could speak to the birds. He had a special bird called Hud-Hud who informed him of the locations of water and was also a special ambassador to different countries. He was given such miracles to the extent that he could even communicate with the ants. The incident is described in the Holy Qur'ān:

حَتّٰى إِذَا أَتَوْا عَلٰى وَادِ النَّمْلِ قَالَتْ نَمْلَةٌ يَا أَيُّهَا النَّمْلُ ادْخُلُوْا مَسَاكِنَكُمْ لَا يَحْطِمَنَّكُمْ سُلَيْمَانُ وَجُنُوْدُهٗ وَهُمْ لَا يَشْعُرُوْنَ

"Till they came to the valley of the ants, one of the ants said: "O' ants! Enter your dwellings lest Sulaimān and his army crush you, while they perceive not (through unawareness)." (27:18)

So, Sayyidunā Sulaimān ﷺ smiled, amazed at her speech (the speech of the ant). Allāmah Zamakshari ﷺ says, Sayyidunā Sulaimān ﷺ heard the ant speak from a distance of three miles.

Sulaimān had a throne which flew in the air. The throne had human beings, Jinns and animals on it. Birds flew on top of him for his shade and shelter. He could travel a journey of two months in one day. The Holy Qur'ān says:

وَلِسُلَيْمَانَ الرِّيْحَ غُدُوُّهَا شَهْرٌ وَرَوَاحُهَا شَهْرٌ وَأَسَلْنَا لَهٗ عَيْنَ الْقِطْرِ وَمِنَ الْجِنِّ مَنْ يَّعْمَلُ بَيْنَ يَدَيْهِ بِإِذْنِ رَبِّهٖ وَمَنْ يَّزِغْ مِنْهُمْ عَنْ أَمْرِنَا نُذِقْهُ مِنْ عَذَابِ السَّعِيْرِ

"Sulaimān, We subjected the wind, its morning stride from sunrise till mid-noon was a month's journey and its afternoon stride

from the mid-day decline of the sun to the sunset was a month's journey. And We caused a fountain of molten brass to flow for him. And there were Jinns that worked in front of him by the permission of his Lord. And whosoever of them turned aside from Our command, We shall cause him to taste the torment of the blazing fire." (34:12)

The Holy Qur'ān further states:

يَعْمَلُوْنَ مَا يَشَآءُ مِنْ مَّحَارِيْبَ وَ تَمَاثِيْلَ وَ جِفَانٍ كَالْجَوَابِ وَقُدُوْرٍ رّٰسِيٰتٍ

"They worked for him as he desired (making) high rooms (mansions) images, and basins as large as reservoirs and cooking pots (cauldrons) fixed (in their places)." (34:13)

6. Miracles of Sayyidunā Mūsā 鬯

Ibn Kathīr 鬯 writes: Miracles were given in accordance to that age and era. During the era of Sayyidunā Mūsā 鬯, sorcery, witchcraft and black magic reached its peak. Thus Allāh 鬯 gifted Sayyidunā Mūsā 鬯 with the staff (the stick) which when he threw it, it transformed into a big serpent.

A challenge took place against 70,000 magicians. It was such a tremendous miracle that the staff of Sayyidunā Mūsā 鬯 turned into an enormous serpent and swallowed all the snakes and serpents made by the magicians' magic. He was also given the glowing hand. Whenever he pressed his right hand to the left side of his chest, it came forth white and shining with no pain.

7. Miracles of Sayyidunā Īsā ﷺ

At the time of Sayyidunā Īsā ﷺ, Tibb (the science of medicine) was prevalent. Sayyidunā Īsā ﷺ was bestowed with curing the lepers and healing those born blind. Allāh ﷻ says in the Holy Qur'ān:

أَنِّيْ اَخْلُقُ لَكُمْ مِّنَ الطِّيْنِ كَهَيْئَةِ الطَّيْرِ فَأَنْفُخُ فِيْهِ فَيَكُوْنُ طَيْرًا بِإِذْنِ اللّٰهِ وَأُبْرِئُ الْأَكْمَهَ وَالْأَبْرَصَ وَأُحْيِ الْمَوْتٰى بِإِذْنِ اللّٰهِ وَأُنَبِّئُكُمْ بِمَا تَأْكُلُوْنَ وَمَا تَدَّخِرُوْنَ فِيْ بُيُوْتِكُمْ

"I make for you out of clay a figure like that of a bird, then breath into it, and so it becomes a bird by Allāh's permission. I heal him who was born blind and the leper, and I bring the dead to life by Allāh's permission. And I inform you of what you eat and what you store in your houses." (3:49)

8. Miracles of the Holy Prophet ﷺ

The Holy Prophet's ﷺ era was the era of poetry, eloquence and literacy. Poetry was so widespread in the society that a book called 'Al Muallaqātus Saba', which is taught in the Islamic schools and is regarded as one of the finest books of eloquent Arabic, was written in gold and hung on the door of the Ka'bah, challenging the whole world to bring something similar. Poetry was so popular that children or even ordinary shepherds could recite hundreds of couplets of poetry spontaneously without any difficulty.

So according to the general trend of the time, Allāh ﷻ revealed the Holy Qur'ān, which is the miracle of miracles because all the other miracles finished with the demise of the Prophets ﷺ.

Sayyidunā Sālih's ☙ miracle, the she-camel went away with his death. Sayyidunā Dāwūd's ☙ miracles finished with his death. Sayyidunā Sulaimān's ☙ miracles of speaking to the birds and animals finished with his death. Sayyidunā Mūsā's ☙ staff and glowing hand finished with his death. Sayyidunā Īsā's ☙ ability of curing the blind and lepers finished when he left the world.

But the Holy Qur'ān was a miracle in the past, it is a miracle in the present time, and it will remain a miracle until the last day. It challenged mankind more than 1400 years ago and it still stands to challenge today.

Qur'anic Challenge

Open the Holy Qur'ān! It proclaims:

قُلْ لَّئِنِ اجْتَمَعَتِ الْإِنْسُ وَالْجِنُّ عَلَى أَنْ يَّأْتُوْا بِمِثْلِ هٰذَا الْقُرْاٰنِ لَا يَأْتُوْنَ بِمِثْلِهِ وَلَوْ كَانَ بَعْضُهُمْ لِبَعْضٍ ظَهِيْرًا

"Say: If mankind and the Jinns joined together to try to produce the like of this Qur'ān, they could not produce the like thereof, even if they helped one another." (17:88)

When the challenge of producing a book like the Holy Qur'ān was seen as impossible, the Lord of the heavens and the earth made the challenge easier by proclaiming:

اَمْ يَقُوْلُوْنَ افْتَرٰىهُ قُلْ فَأْتُوْا بِعَشْرِ سُوَرٍ مِّثْلِهِ مُفْتَرَيٰتٍ وَّادْعُوْا مَنِ اسْتَطَعْتُمْ مِّنْ دُوْنِ اللّٰهِ اِنْ كُنْتُمْ صٰدِقِيْنَ

"Do they say He (Prophet Muhammad) forged it (the Qur'ān).

Say: Bring ten forged Sūrahs (chapters) like unto it, and call whosoever you can other than Allāh (for your help) if you speak the truth." (11:13)

The challenge is then made even easier. Allāh ﷻ says:

وَإِن كُنتُمْ فِى رَيْبٍ مِّمَّا نَزَّلْنَا عَلَى عَبْدِنَا فَأْتُوا بِسُورَةٍ مِّن مِّثْلِهِ

"And if you (Polytheists, Jews and Christians) are in doubt concerning that which We sent down (Qur'ān) to our servant (Muhammad) then produce a chapter of the like thereof". (2:23)

Inspite of all the challenges presented, the Holy Qur'ān states:

فَإِن لَّمْ تَفْعَلُوا وَلَن تَفْعَلُوا فَاتَّقُوا النَّارَ الَّتِى وَقُودُهَا النَّاسُ وَالْحِجَارَةُ أُعِدَّتْ لِلْكَافِرِينَ

"But if you do not do it and indeed you can never do it, then fear the fire of Hell whose fuel is men and stones, prepared for the disbelievers." (2:24)

The challenge is still outstanding today and it will remain so till the last day. No one can even bring three verses equal to Sūrah Al-Kawthar or Sūrah Al-Asr.

When Musailamah Kazzāb (the impostor) claimed prophethood during the era of the Holy Prophet ﷺ, his supporters called upon him to meet the challenge. After long meditation and many months of hard work he came out with: Elephant; what is an elephant? Do you know what is an elephant? It has a long trunk and a short tail.

Any sane person can see the stupidity and futility of this impostor. The Holy Qur'ān is still in its original text, not a single word or a single letter has been changed till this day, and there will be no change till the last day. Inshā-Allāh.

The enemies of Islām have made many attempts to change the Holy Qur'ān, but in vain. They have been unsuccessful. How can they change the Holy Qur'ān, when Allāh 🕮 has preserved the Holy Qur'ān Himself? Allāh 🕮 says in the Holy Qur'ān:

$$\text{اِنَّا نَحْنُ نَزَّلْنَا الذِّكْرَ وَاِنَّا لَهُ لَحٰفِظُوْنَ}$$

"We have revealed the Holy Qur'ān and We will safeguard it (from corruption)." (15:9)

An Inspiring Incident

During the time of Mamūn Rashīd, who was the leader of the Muslim world, there was an annual gathering where people of different sects and different religions would come and participate. In one such gathering there was a Jew who spoke fluently and eloquently. Mamūn Rashīd being very impressed by his speech called him and invited him to accept Islām but he refused. The following year, the same Jew attended the gathering but this time not as a Jew, but as a Muslim, and he spoke with great knowledge of Islām. Mamūn Rashīd surprised at his acceptance of Islām, called him and said, "What made you accept Islām now? When I invited you last year, you refused."

He thus narrated his incident, "After I went from the gathering last year, I decided to test the authenticity of all religions. I was a prolific and gifted writer, so I wrote three copies of the Tawrah, three copies of the Bible and three copies of the Holy Qur'ān. I made some alterations in all of them. Then, in turn I took the three copies of the Tawrah to the Synagogue and presented them to the Rabbis to purchase them. The Rabbis happily purchased the Tawrahs with a considerable amount of money and they appreciated the work.

I then took the three copies of the Bible to the church and showed them to the priests. They also purchased the Bibles for a good price. Finally, I took the three copies of the Holy Qur'ān and I presented them to the scholars of Islām but they refused and became very angry and remarked, "This is not a copy of the original Holy Qur'ān, you have tampered and altered the Holy Qur'ān, go away, until you do not bring us a copy of the original, we shall not purchase it."

Thus, I embraced Islām knowing that Islām is the only true religion because it's religious book is so authentic and preserved.

Status of the Holy Qur'ān

We Muslims have neglected the Holy Qur'ān. We have forgotten the importance and the significance of the Holy Qur'ān and removed it from our hearts. Allāh ﷻ says:

لَوْ اَنْزَلْنَا هٰذَا الْقُرْاٰنَ عَلٰى جَبَلٍ لَّرَاَيْتَهٗ خَاشِعًا مُّتَصَدِّعًا مِّنْ خَشْيَةِ اللهِ

"Had We sent down this Holy Qur'ān on a mountain, you would surely have seen it humbling itself and rent asunder by the fear

of Allāh." (59:21)

A Hadīth can be found in Sahīh Al-Bukhāri narrated by Sayyidunā Jābir Ibn Abdullāh ﷺ, who said: The Holy Prophet ﷺ used to stand by a palm tree on Fridays. An Ansāri woman or man said, "O Allāh's Messenger ﷺ! Shall we make a pulpit for you?" He replied, "If you wish." So they made a pulpit for him and when it was Friday, he proceeded towards the pulpit for delivering the Khutbah (sermon). The palm tree started crying like a child, the Holy Prophet ﷺ descended (from the pulpit) and embraced it while it continued mourning like a child being comforted. The Holy Prophet ﷺ said, "It was crying and yearning for what it used to hear of religious knowledge given near it."

On another occasion the Holy Prophet ﷺ was in a place called Batn -Nakhla. He recited the Holy Qur'ān. The Jinns came and listened attentively. They said:

$$\text{اِنَّا سَمِعْنَا قُرْاٰنًا عَجَبًا}$$

"Indeed, We have heard an astonishing Qur'ān." (72:1)

$$\text{يَّهْدِيْ اِلَى الرُّشْدِ فَاٰمَنَّا بِهٖ وَلَنْ نُّشْرِكَ بِرَبِّنَا اَحَدًا}$$

"It guides to the Right Path, and we have believed therein, and we shall never join (in worship) anything with our lord (Allāh)."(72:2)

The Holy Qur'ān was so inspiring for them. Thus, all the Jinns in the gathering accepted Islām.

Sayyidunā Umar's ⬥ Acceptance of Islām

Virtually everyone knows how Sayyidunā Umar ⬥ accepted Islām. Before the acceptance of Islām he made the firm intention to assassinate the Holy Prophet ﷺ. He went furiously towards the Holy Prophet's ﷺ house. On the way he met Sayyidunā Nu'aim Ibn Abdullāh ⬥ who stopped him and enquired where he was going in this angry state. He replied, "I am going to put an end to this person who has caused corruption in our community." Sayyidunā Nu'aim Ibn Abdullāh ⬥ shocked and terrified, remarked, "Take care of your sister and brother-in-law, they have also accepted Islām." Sayyidunā Umar's ⬥ anger increased manifold. He turned direction towards his sister's house and when he arrived, he forcefully entered the house. He got hold of his brother-in-law and sister and beat them severely. "You have accepted Islām," he shouted. The sister of Sayyidunā Umar ⬥ was no ordinary woman. After all she was the sister of Umar. She spoke boldly and said, "Yes, we have accepted Islām. Do whatever you like, we will not leave Islām!" The verses of Sūrah Tā-hā was left in the room by mistake and the eyes of Sayyidunā Umar ⬥ fell on them. He began reading and tears started flowing from his eyes. He recited Tā-hā and each word began to inspire him. It was melting his heart. He then recited the Kalimah. Let us now rectify ourselves and ponder upon the Holy Qur'ān.

Before I conclude my talk, I would like to mention two rights the

Holy Qur'ān has over us. Firstly, we should recite the Holy Qur'ān on a regular basis. Many of us do not recite the Holy Qur'ān. After we have left the Maktab, we have probably not opened the Holy Qur'ān since. Many of us have forgotten how to read the Holy Qur'ān. For most of us the only time we open the Holy Qur'ān is when one of our beloved pass away. Remember my brothers and sisters, the Holy Qur'ān has not come to be put on the highest shelf of our house, nor has it come to be recited only at the time of grief and sorrow. But the Holy Qur'ān has come as a solution and a remedy for all time. Allāh ﷻ says:

مَا فَرَّطْنَا فِى الْكِتَابِ مِنْ شَيْءٍ

"We have not missed anything in the book." (6:38)

All our problems will be solved once we start practicing upon the Holy Qur'ān, and this is the second important thing I would like to mention. We should act upon the commandments of the Holy Qur'ān. Our pious elders and forefathers acted upon the Holy Qur'ān and they became glittering stars in this world and the hereafter.

A Thought Provoking Incident

The great Sayyidunā Umar Fārūq ؓ, look at his life! It is stated in the Hadīth of Bukhāri that a person called Uwainah Ibn Hisn once came to his nephew Hur Ibn Qais ؓ who was a close person of Sayyidunā Umar ؓ. He requested his nephew, Hur Ibn Qais ؓ (due to the fact that he held a great status in the eyes of Sayyidunā Umar ؓ) to ask permission so that he can come and sit in his gathering. His nephew Hur Ibn Qais ﷺ, asked for permission which was granted. His uncle came and ignorantly uttered, "O' son of Khattāb you do not give us booty, you do not give us what is due to us, and you do not judge justly." Sayyidunā Umar ﷺ hearing this became very angry and he had the right to become angry because of his innocence. His justice was well known in the Muslim world. He was ready to pounce with fury, when the Holy Qur'ān intervened. Hur Ibn Qais ﷺ recited the verse:

$$ خُذِ الْعَفْوَ وَأْمُرْ بِالْعُرْفِ وَاَعْرِضْ عَنِ الْجَاهِلِيْنَ $$

"Show forgiveness, enjoin what is good and turn away from the foolish (i.e. don't punish them)." (7:199)

The narrator says, hearing the verse of the Holy Qur'ān Sayyidunā Umar ﷺ abruptly halted, his anger subdued and he sat down.

Let us attach the Holy Qur'ān to every aspect of our life, like the Sahābah ﷺ did. Then Allāh ﷻ will give success to us in this world and the hereafter like the way He gave the Companions of the Holy Prophet ﷺ.

Revelation *of* the
Holy Qur'ān

أُتْلُ مَآ أُوْحِیَ اِلَیْكَ مِنَ الْكِتَابِ وَ اَقِمِ الصَّلٰوةَ

"Recite that which has been revealed to you from the book,
and establish Salāh." (29:45)

Connection with the Holy Qur'ān

We as Muslims believe in the Holy Qur'ān. We believe the Holy Qur'ān to be the final revelation sent by Allāh ﷻ to His beloved Prophet ﷺ. But let us look into our lives. How much impact, how much influence and how much affect does the Holy Qur'ān have in our lives? Are we abiding by all the laws ordered by Allāh ﷻ or are we following our own carnal desires? We can judge this for ourselves. Every person who has true Imān is responsible of establishing a connection with the Holy Qur'ān by reciting the Holy Qur'ān, understanding the Holy Qur'ān and implementing the commands of the Holy Qur'ān into one's daily life.

Recitation of the Holy Qur'ān

The recitation of the Holy Qur'ān either with understanding or without understanding are both acts of worship. As a result of recitation a strong connection is established between Allāh ﷻ and the reader. In Sūrah Al-Ankabut, Allāh ﷻ has commanded the believers to recite the Holy Qur'ān. He states,

$$ اُتْلُ مَآ أُوْحِيَ إِلَيْكَ مِنَ الْكِتَابِ وَ أَقِمِ الصَّلٰوةَ $$

"Recite that which has been revealed to you from the book and establish Salāh." (29:45)

Imām Tirmizi ﷺ records a Hadīth in his Sunan regarding the reward of mere recital without understanding. Sayyidunā Abdullāh Ibn Mas'ūd ﷺ says that Rasūlullāh ﷺ said, "Whoever recites one

24

letter from the Holy Qur'ān, there is for him a reward for it, and every good deed is multiplied ten times. I do not say that Alif Lām Mīm is a letter. Rather Alif is a letter, Lām is a letter and Mīm is a letter."

Dream of Imām Ahmad Ibn Hanbal 卐

Imām Ahmad Ibn Hanbal 卐, one of the four great Imāms said, "I saw Allāh 卐 in my dream and asked him, "O' my Sustainer, how have those who have drawn near to You achieved this nearness?" Allāh 卐 replied, "It is achieved by My speech (in other words by the Holy Qur'ān) O' Ahmad!" Imām Ahmad Ibn Hanbal 卐 said, "I enquired, O' my Sustainer, is it by understanding Your speech or without understanding it?" Allāh 卐 replied, "By understanding as well as without understanding."

However an earnest effort must be made to understand the Holy Qur'ān. Allāh 卐 stresses this point. Thus He says:

$$كِتٰبٌ اَنْزَلْنٰهُ اِلَيْكَ مُبٰرَكٌ لِّيَدَّبَّرُوْٓا اٰيٰتِه وَلِيَتَذَكَّرَ اُولُوا الْاَلْبَابِ$$

"A book We have revealed to you, it is blessed, so that the people ponder over its verses and so that the intelligent are admonished." (38:29)

Thirdly, every effort must be made to act upon the teachings of the Holy Qur'ān. To do this, it is compulsory and imperative that we are acquainted with the Holy Qur'ān, so that we know the laws of Islām. Allāh 卐 says in Sūrah Al-An'ām:

وَهَذَا كِتَابٌ اَنْزَلْنَهُ مُبَرَكٌ فَاتَّبِعُوهُ وَاتَّقُوْا لَعَلَّكُمْ تُرْحَمُوْنَ

"This is a book We have revealed, full of blessing, so follow it and abstain from wrong doing so you are blessed." (6:155)

Our Neglect

In this temporary world when we intend to meet an important person, a prominent figure, we make proper and adequate preparations. We make sure that we are well dressed. We have a bath, apply perfume on our bodies and prepare in advance what we are going to say to him. But alas, when the matter is regarding the Dīn, attending the Masjid or the Madrasah, to sit and recite the Glorious Qur'ān, we hardly bother about cleanliness. We are so careless and neglectful that even at the time of reciting the Holy Qur'ān , we are gazing around everywhere. We speak between the recitals whilst keeping the Holy Qur'ān open. This is highly disrespectful. Why is this our attitude? Do we not realize who we are conversing with? We are in actual fact, in reality, speaking directly to the Creator, my Creator, your Creator, the Creator of the heavens and the earth. Let us inculcate the teachings of the Holy Qur'ān in our hearts, the greatest miracle given to any Prophet.

Types of Wahī (Revelation)

Have we ever wondered, how this Holy Qur'ān has come to us from Allāh ﷻ? Before I answer this, I would like to explain how Allah ﷻ communicates with His Prophets. The Holy Qur'ān tells us:

وَمَا كَانَ لِبَشَرٍ اَنْ يُّكَلِّمَهُ اللهُ اِلَّا وَحْيًا اَوْ مِنْ وَّرَائِ حِجَابٍ
اَوْ يُرْسِلَ رَسُوْلًا فَيُوْحِيَ بِاِذْنِه مَايَشَاءُ اِنَّهُ عَلِيٌّ حَكِيْمٌ

**"It is not possible for any human being that Allāh should speak
to him unless it is by inspiration or from behind a veil or He
sends a messenger (an angel) to reveal what He wills by His permission. Indeed He is All-High and All-Wise." (42:51)**

The three ways Allāh ﷻ communicates with His Prophets are as
follows;

First Type of Waḥī

The first category of revelation is a direct communication by Allāh
ﷻ with His Prophets. No words are exchanged. Allāh ﷻ puts the
revelation into the Prophet's heart and through the knowledge giv-
en by Allāh ﷻ, the Prophet is aware that this is from Allāh ﷻ. A
perfect example of this is the incident of Ibrāhīm ﷺ and Ismāīl
ﷺ. Sayyidunā Ibrāhīm ﷺ is commanded by Allāh ﷻ through direct Waḥī to sacrifice his child. The command is:

يٰبُنَيَّ اِنِّيْ اَرٰى فِى الْمَنَامِ اَنِّيْ اَذْبَحُكَ فَانْظُرْ مَاذَا تَرٰى

**"O' my son! I have seen in a dream that I am slaughtering you
(offering you in sacrifice to Allāh) so tell me what you
think." (37:102)**

قَالَ يٰاَبَتِ افْعَلْ مَا تُؤْمَرُ سَتَجِدُنِيْ اِنْ شَاءَ اللهُ مِنَ الصَّابِرِيْنَ

"He said, O' my father! Do what you are commanded, if Allāh

wills, you shall find me from amongst the patient ones".(37:102)

So, this is an example of Wahī which is called Wahī Qalbi.

Second Type of Wahī

The second type of communication with the Prophets is made from behind a veil, or some type of screen. In this method, Allāh ﷻ speaks directly to His Prophets but behind a screen. A clear example of this is the incident of Sayyidunā Mūsā ﷺ. The Holy Qur'ān says:

فَلَمَّا اَتٰهَا نُوْدِيَ يٰمُوْسٰى اِنِّيْ اَنَا رَبُّكَ فَاخْلَعْ نَعْلَيْكَ اِنَّكَ بِالْوَادِ الْمُقَدَّسِ طُوًى

"And when he came to it (the fire) he was called "O Mūsā, verily I am your Lord! So take off your shoes, you are in the sacred valley of Tuwā." (20:11-12)

Third Type of Wahī

The third type of communication is an indirect communication, through the mediation of an angel. The Holy Qur'ān was revealed in this method through an angel named Jibrīl ﷺ.

When the Holy Prophet ﷺ was forty years old, he received the first revelation. The Hadīth can be found in Sahīh Al-Bukhāri. Sayyidah Ā'ishah ﷺ narrates, "The commencement of the divine inspiration to Allāh's Messenger ﷺ was in the form of righteous good (true) dreams, which came true like bright daylight, then the love of seclusion was bestowed upon him."

The First Revelation

The Holy Prophet ﷺ would seclude himself in the cave of Hirā,
where he used to worship Allāh ﷻ alone. Suddenly the truth descended upon him while he was in the cave of Hirā. The Hadīth
regarding this incident says, "The angel (Jibrīl ﷿) came to me and
asked me to read. I replied, 'I do not know how to read.' Then the
angel caught me forcefully and pressed me so hard that I could
not bear it any more. He then released me. Then he again asked me
to read, and I replied, 'I do not know how to read.' Thereupon he
caught me again and pressed me a second time till I could not bear
it any more. He then released me and again asked me to read, but
again I replied, 'I do not know how to read.' Thereupon he caught
me for the third time and pressed me, and then released me and
said:

اِقْرَأْ بِاسْمِ رَبِّكَ الَّذِى خَلَقَ خَلَقَ الْإِنْسَانَ مِنْ عَلَقٍ اِقْرَأْ وَرَبُّكَ الْاَكْرَمُ
الَّذِى عَلَّمَ بِالْقَلَمِ عَلَّمَ الْاِنْسَانَ مَا لَمْ يَعْلَمْ

**"Read in the name of your Lord, Who has created (all that exists).
He has created man from a clot of blood. Read, your Lord is the
Most Generous Who taught with the pen, taught mankind what
he knew not." (96:1-5)**

Then Allāh's Messenger ﷺ returned with the revelation and with
his heart beating anxiously. He went to his beloved wife Khadījah
﵂ and said, "Cover me, Cover me." She covered him till his anxiety was over. After that, he informed her everything that had tran-
spired and said, "I fear that something may happen to me." Say-

yidah Khadījah ﷺ replied, "Never! By Allāh ﷻ, Allāh ﷻ will never disgrace you. You keep good relations with your kith and kin. You help the poor and the destitute, and you serve your guests generously and you assist the afflicted ones." The incident continues that Sayyidah Khadījah ﷺ then accompanied the Holy Prophet ﷺ to her cousin Waraqah Ibn Nawfal, who during the period of ignorance became a Christian and used to write the scriptures in Hebrew. He would write from the Gospel in Hebrew as much as Allāh ﷻ wished him to write. He was an old man and had lost his eyesight. Sayyidah Khadījah ﷺ said to him, "O my cousin, listen to the story of your nephew."

Waraqah asked, "My nephew, what have you seen?" Allāh's Messenger ﷺ described what he had seen. Waraqah said, "This is the same one who keeps the secrets i.e. angel Jibrīl ﷺ, whom Allāh ﷻ had sent to Mūsā ﷺ. I wish I were young and I could live up to the time when your people will turn you out." Allāh's Messenger ﷺ asked in astonishment, "Will they drive me out?"

He replied in the affirmative and said, "Anyone who came with something similar to what you have brought was treated with hostility and if I shall remain alive till the day (when you will be turned out) then I will support you strongly." A few days later, Waraqah died. Divine revelation came to a pause which was a source of further anxiety for the Holy Prophet ﷺ.

The Second Revelation

Regarding the second revelation, the Hadīth can be found in Sahīh Al-Bukhari, narrated by Sayyidunā Jābir Ibn Abdullāh ؓ that the Holy Prophet ﷺ said, "While I was walking, all of a sudden I heard a voice from the sky. I looked up and saw the same Angel (Jibrīl ﷷ) who had visited me at the cave of Hirā, sitting on a chair between the sky and the earth. I was shocked seeing him and came back home and said wrap me (in blankets), and then Allāh ﷻ revealed the following verses:

يَاأَيُّهَاالْمُدَّثِّرُ قُمْ فَأَنْذِرْ وَرَبَّكَ فَكَبِّرْ وَثِيَابَكَ فَطَهِّرْ وَالرُّجْزَ فَاهْجُرْ

"O' you enveloped in garments, arise and warn. Proclaim the greatness of your Lord. Keep your clothes clean and keep away from idols." (74:1-5)

In the beginning, the Holy Prophet ﷺ would bear the revelation with great stress and hardship and used to move his lips quickly with the revelation in order to avoid forgetting it. Hence Allāh ﷻ revealed the following verses:

لَا تُحَرِّكْ بِهِ لِسَانَكَ لِتَعْجَلَ بِهِ إِنَّ عَلَيْنَا جَمْعَهُ وَقُرْآنَهُ

"Move not your tongue concerning the Qur'ān (O' Muhammad) to make haste therewith. It is for Us to collect it and give to you. (The ability to recite the Holy Qur'ān and memorize it)" (75:16-17)

فَإِذَا قَرَأْنَاهُ فَاتَّبِعْ قُرْآنَهُ ثُمَّ إِنَّ عَلَيْنَا بَيَانَهُ

31

"So when We have recited it (to you) then follow its recital. Then it is for Us (Allāh) to make it clear to you." (75:18-19)

After that Allāh's Messenger ﷺ used to listen to Jibrīl ﷺ whenever he came and after his departure, he would recite it as Jibrīl ﷺ had recited it.

Duration of Revelation

In this way, Allāh ﷻ revealed the verses of the Holy Qur'ān. Whenever the need arose he sent the revelation. Sometimes one Sūrah, sometimes a few verses, sometimes one verse, sometimes a portion of a verse would be revealed. It took approximately 23 years for the entire Holy Qur'ān to be revealed to the Holy Prophet ﷺ.

A Question

Now let me divert your attention towards a question that commonly arises. From some verses of the Holy Qur'ān there is an indication that the Holy Qur'ān was revealed at once and not gradually. The verses which indicate this point are:

إِنَّا أَنْزَلْنَاهُ فِى لَيْلَةِ الْقَدْرِ

"Indeed We have revealed it (the Holy Qur'ān) in the night of Power, (in the night of Qadr)." (97:1)

This verse expresses that it was revealed in Lailatul Qadr. Another verse can be found in Sūrah Ad-Dukhān:

اِنَّا اَنْزَلْنٰهُ فِیْ لَیْلَةٍ مُّبٰرَکَةٍ

"Indeed We have revealed it (the Holy Qur'ān) in the blessed night." (44:3)

Yet in other verses, it indicates that the Holy Qur'ān was revealed in stages, portion by portion, for example, in one verse Allāh ﷻ says:

وَقَالَ الَّذِیْنَ کَفَرُوْا لَوْ لَا نُزِّلَ عَلَیْهِ الْقُرْاٰنُ جُمْلَةً وَّاحِدَةً

"Those who disbelieve say, 'Why is not the Qur'ān revealed to him all at once?" (25:32)

The reason for their objection was that the previous Kitābs; Injīl, Tawrah and Zabūr were revealed at once. Therefore why was the Holy Qur'ān not revealed at once as well. But Allāh ﷻ says:

کَذٰلِكَ لِنُثَبِّتَ بِهِ فُؤَادَكَ وَرَتَّلْنٰهُ تَرْتِیْلًا

"Thus (it is sent down in parts) so that We may strengthen your heart thereby. And We have revealed it to you gradually." (25:32)

In another verse, Allāh ﷻ says:

وَقُرْاٰنًا فَرَقْنٰهُ لِتَقْرَاَهٗ عَلَی النَّاسِ عَلٰی مُکْثٍ وَّنَزَّلْنٰهُ تَنْزِیْلًا

"And it is the Qur'ān, which We have divided (into parts) in order that you might recite it to men at intervals and We have revealed it by stages." (17:106)

33

These verses seem to be contradictory, but in reality there is no contradiction in the Holy Qur'ān. The answer is that the Holy Qur'ān was revealed twice. Yes, it was revealed twice! Once from the Lawh Mahfūz (preserved tablet) to the first heaven, and then from the first heaven to the Holy Prophet ﷺ.

Thus, the Holy Qur'ān was initially revealed all at once from the Lawh Mahfūz to the first heaven. So the verses of Sūrah Al-Qadr and Sūrah Ad-Dukhān relate to the revelation from the preserved tablet to the first heaven, which occurred all at once.

The other verses of the Holy Qur'ān, where it is mentioned that the Holy Qur'ān was revealed in stages and intervals relates to the revelation of the Holy Qur'ān i.e. from the first heaven to the Holy Prophet ﷺ.

The Wisdom Behind the Revelation in Stages

You may ask: Why was it revealed in stages and not all at once like the previous divine books? The scholars have given many reasons; One reason is so as to gradually implement the laws of Islām on the people of that time. As you may know the state of the people in the Days of Ignorance was such that if all the commandments, orders and laws were revealed at once, it would have been virtually impossible for them to act upon the Holy Qur'ān. For example the following orders:

أَقِيْمُوا الصَّلٰوةَ وَاٰتُوا الزَّكٰوةَ

"Establish Salāh and give Zakāt." (2:43)

يٰأَيُّهَا الَّذِينَ اٰمَنُوا كُتِبَ عَلَيْكُمُ الصِّيَامُ

"O' people who believe, fasting is compulsory on you." (2:183)

وَلِلّٰهِ عَلَى النَّاسِ حِجُّ البَيْتِ مَنِ اسْتَطَاعَ اِلَيْهِ سَبِيلاً

"And Hajj (pilgrimage to Makkah) to the house of Allāh, is a duty that mankind owes to Allāh for those who can afford the expenses." (3:97)

Another reason is to make it easy to memorize and understand. Due to the fact that it was revealed in portions, it was easy to commit to memory and it was easily understood.

Three Methods of Preserving the Holy Qur'ān

At the time of the Holy Prophet ﷺ, three methods were used to preserve the Holy Qur'ān.

Firstly: Hifz – to memorize whatever was revealed. The Sahābah ﷺ had amazing memories with which they memorized the Holy Qur'ān.

Secondly: At-Ta'āmul – to act upon whatever was revealed. The Sahābah ﷺ acted upon everything that was revealed.

Thirdly: Al-Kitābah – to write whatever was revealed. Some Sahābah ﷺ who knew how to write, wrote the verses of the Holy Qur'ān. Whenever verses were revealed, the Holy Prophet ﷺ would call his Companions who knew how to read and write, and he used to dictate to them and the Sahābah ﷺ would write it on bones, palm leaves, paper or whatever was available at that time. He then used to instruct them to put the verses in a certain Sūrah, in a specific order. In this way, the Holy Qur'ān was verified and checked completely in the presence of the Holy Prophet ﷺ.

Before commencing the Tafsīr of Sūrah Al-Fātihah, I would like to speak briefly about Ta'awwudh (A'ūdhu-billāhiminashaytānir rajīm) and Tasmiyah (Bismillāhir-Rahmānir Rahīm).

Rules Regarding Ta'awwudh

Ta'awwudh is not a verse of the Holy Qur'ān but before we commence the Holy Qur'ān it is compulsory to recite Ta'awwudh. The Holy Qur'ān says:

$$\text{فَاِذَا قَرَاْتَ الْقُرْاٰنَ فَاسْتَعِذْ بِاللّٰهِ مِنَ الشَّيْطَانِ الرَّجِيْمِ}$$

"When you commence to recite the Holy Qur'ān then seek refuge in Allāh from the cursed Shaytān." (16:98)

Thus, it is important to recite Ta'awwudh before we start the Holy Qur'ān from any place. If we stop at any place, we should start by reciting the Holy Qur'ān with Ta'awwudh again.

Rules Regarding Tasmiyah

In pre-Islamic Arabia, it was a custom of the people to begin every work by mentioning the names of their idols. In order to abolish this ignorant way, Jibrīl عليه السلام brought the first verse of the Holy

Qur'ān in which the command is given to begin the Holy Qur'ān with the Name of Allāh 🌸.

اِقۡرَأۡ بِاسۡمِ رَبِّكَ الَّذِیۡ خَلَقَ

"Read in the name of your Lord Who created." (96:1)

The great scholar Imām Jalāl Uddīn Suyūti 🌸 has mentioned that all the revealed books begin in the name of Allāh 🌸. Some Ulamā are of the opinion that Bismillāhir Rahmānir Rahīm is exclusive to the Holy Qur'ān and the Ummah of Muhammad 🌸.

Both these views are possible in that all revealed books begin in the Name of Allāh 🌸, but the Holy Qur'ān begins in the Name of Allāh 🌸 with these exclusive words. Even before this verse was revealed, Rasūlullāh 🌸 began everything by saying, **Bismikallāhumma (O' Allāh I begin in Your Name)."**

The Ahādīth exhorts the beginning of every matter with the Name of Allāh 🌸. Rasūlullāh 🌸 has said, "Every important matter that starts without Bismillāh is not blessed". In one Hadīth it is mentioned that when closing the door of the house say Bismillāh. When extinguishing the lamp say Bismillāh. When covering utensils (in which there is food) say Bismillāh. The Holy Qur'ān and Ahādīth have mentioned the saying of Bismillāh when beginning to eat, drink, perform Wudhu and when boarding and alighting from transport.

Bismillāh is used to mean one of three things;
1.   For Musāhabah (to attach Allāh's 🌸 Name to ones action).

As in to begin with Allāh's ﷻ Name.

2. For Istiānah (to seek assistance from Allāh ﷻ). As in to begin in Allāh's ﷻ Name seeking His assistance.

3. For Tabarruk (to seek blessings). As in to begin in Allāh's ﷻ Name seeking His blessings.

The Script of Bismillāh

The script of Bismillāh itself is unique and is maintained as it was written in the copy of the Holy Qur'ān of Sayyidunā Uthmān ؓ. According to the grammar of the Arabic language, Bismillāh should be written with a Hamzah after the letter Bā, but because in the Holy Qur'ān of Sayyidunā Uthmān ؓ the letter Bā was joined to the letter Sīn without a Hamzah, this script has been preserved up to the present day.

Ar-Rahmān and Ar-Rahīm (the Most Beneficent, the Most Merciful)

Ar-Rahmān and Ar-Rahīm are attributes of Allāh ﷻ. Ar-Rahmān being the One Who is Merciful unto all things created and still to be created. Like the word 'Allāh ﷻ,' this word too is exclusively for Allāh ﷻ alone since none other can have these qualities. The words 'Allāh ﷻ' and 'Rahmān' do not have dual or plural forms.

'Ar-Rahīm' means the being whose mercy is complete. The word 'Rahīm' could be used for others too, just as it is used for Rasūlullāh ﷺ in the Holy Qur'ān where Allāh ﷻ says in Sūrah At-

Tawbah,

بِالْمُؤْمِنِيْنَ رَءُوْفٌ رَّحِيْمٌ

"To the believers he is most compassionate and merciful." (9:128)

It is clear from this explanation that it is unlawful and sinful to call a person only Rahmān or in an abbreviation (abridged) or corrupted form in place of Abdur Rahmān or Fadhlur Rahmān.

Some Masā'il Regarding Ta'awwudh and Tasmiyah

It is compulsory to read 'Ta'awwudh' and then 'Tasmiyah' when beginning the recitation of the Holy Qur'ān. It is also compulsory to recite 'Ta'awwudh' and 'Tasmiyah' at the beginning of all Sūrahs of the Holy Qur'ān except in Sūrah Barā'ah (Sūrah At-Tawbah).

Since Bismillāhir Rahmānir Rahīm is a verse of Sūrah An-Naml and also a separate verse between the Sūrahs, all laws of recital, touching and handling are similar to that of the Holy Qur'ān. Hence it is not permissible to touch that paper or article on which a verse is written without Wudhu, or when a woman is in state of Haidh (menstruation) or Nifās (post-natal bleeding). The one who is in a state of Haidh or Nifās may read Bismillāh as a Du'ā, but not as recitation of a verse of the Holy Qur'ān.

With these few Masā'il, I would like to conclude my speech. May Allāh 🕮 give us the correct understanding of the Holy Qur'ān.

Other titles from JKN Publications

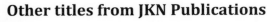

Your Questions Answered

An outstanding book written by Shaykh Mufti Saiful Islām. A very comprehensive yet simple Fatāwa book and a source of guidance that reaches out to a wider audience i.e. the English speaking Muslims. The reader will benefit from the various answers to questions based on the Laws of Islām relating to the beliefs of Islām, knowledge, Sunnah, pillars of Islām, marriage, divorce and contemporary issues.

UK RRP: £7.50

Hadeeth for Beginners

A concise Hadeeth book with various Ahādeeth that relate to basic Ibādāh and moral etiquettes in Islām accessible to a wider readership. Each Hadeeth has been presented with the Arabic text, its translation and commentary to enlighten the reader, its meaning and application in day-to-day life.

UK RRP: £3.00

Du'ā for Beginners

This book contains basic Du'ās which every Muslim should recite on a daily basis. Highly recommended to young children and adults studying at Islamic schools and Madrasahs so that one may cherish the beautiful treasure of supplications of our beloved Prophet ﷺ in one's daily life, which will ultimately bring peace and happiness in both worlds, Inshā-Allāh.

UK RRP: £2.00

How well do you know Islām?

An exciting educational book which contains 300 multiple questions and answers to help you increase your knowledge on Islām! Ideal for the whole family, especially children and adult students to learn new knowledge in an enjoyable way and cherish the treasures of knowledge that you will acquire from this book. A very beneficial tool for educational syllabus.

UK RRP: £3.00

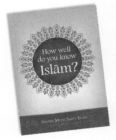

Treasures of the Holy Qur'ān

This book entitled "Treasures of the Holy Qur'ān" has been compiled to create a stronger bond between the Holy Qur'ān and the readers. It mentions the different virtues of Sūrahs and verses from the Holy Qur'ān with the hope that the readers will increase their zeal and enthusiasm to recite and inculcate the teachings of the Holy Qur'ān into their daily lives.

UK RRP: £3.00

Marriage - A Complete Solution

Islām regards marriage as a great act of worship. This book has been designed to provide the fundamental teachings and guidelines of all what relates to the marital life in a simplified English language. It encapsulates in a nutshell all the marriage laws mentioned in many of the main reference books in order to facilitate their understanding and implementation.

UK RRP: £5.00

Pearls of Luqmān

This book is a comprehensive commentary of Sūrah Luqmān, written beautifully by Shaykh Mufti Saiful Islām. It offers the reader with an enquiring mind, abundance of advice, guidance, counselling and wisdom.

The reader will be enlightened by many wonderful topics and anecdotes mentioned in this book, which will create a greater understanding of the Holy Qur'ān and its wisdom. The book highlights some of the wise sayings and words of advice Luqmān ﷺ gave to his son.

UK RRP: £3.00

Arabic Grammar for Beginners

This book is a study of Arabic Grammar based on the subject of Nahw (Syntax) in a simplified English format. If a student studies this book thoroughly, he/she will develop a very good foundation in this field, Inshā-Allāh. Many books have been written on this subject in various languages such as Arabic, Persian and Urdu. However, in this day and age there is a growing demand for this subject to be available in English .

UK RRP: £3.00

A Gift to My Youngsters

This treasure filled book, is a collection of Islamic stories, morals and anecdotes from the life of our beloved Prophet ﷺ, his Companions ؓ and the pious predecessors. The stories and anecdotes are based on moral and ethical values, which the reader will enjoy sharing with their peers, friends, families and loved ones.

"A Gift to My Youngsters" – is a wonderful gift presented to the readers personally, by the author himself, especially with the youngsters in mind. He has carefully selected stories and anecdotes containing beautiful morals, lessons and valuable knowledge and wisdom.

UK RRP: £5.00

Travel Companion

The beauty of this book is that it enables a person on any journey, small or distant or simply at home, to utilise their spare time to read and benefit from an exciting and vast collection of important and interesting Islamic topics and lessons. Written in simple and easy to read text, this book will immensely benefit both the newly interested person in Islām and the inquiring mind of a student expanding upon their existing knowledge. Inspiring reminders from the Holy Qur'ān and the blessed words of our beloved Prophet ﷺ beautifies each topic and will illuminate the heart of the reader. **UK RRP: £5.00**

Pearls of Wisdom

Junaid Baghdādi ﷺ once said, "Allāh ﷻ strengthens through these Islamic stories the hearts of His friends, as proven from the Qur'anic verse,

"And all that We narrate unto you of the stories of the Messengers, so as to strengthen through it your heart." (11:120)

Mālik Ibn Dinār ﷺ stated that such stories are gifts from Paradise. He also emphasised to narrate these stories as much as possible as they are gems and it is possible that an individual might find a truly rare and invaluable gem among them. **UK RRP: £6.00**

Inspirations

This book contains a compilation of selected speeches delivered by Shaykh Mufti Saiful Islām on a variety of topics such as the Holy Qur'ān, Nikāh and eating Halāl. Having previously been compiled in separate booklets, it was decided that the transcripts be gathered together in one book for the benefit of the reader. In addition to this, we have included in this book, further speeches which have not yet been printed.

UK RRP: £6.00

Gift to my Sisters

A thought provoking compilation of very interesting articles including real life stories of pious predecessors, imaginative illustrations and much more. All designed to influence and motivate mothers, sisters, wives and daughters towards an ideal Islamic lifestyle. A lifestyle referred to by our Creator, Allāh ﷻ in the Holy Qur'ān as the means to salvation and ultimate success.

UK RRP: £6.00

Gift to my Brothers

A thought provoking compilation of very interesting articles including real life stories of pious predecessors, imaginative illustrations, medical advices on intoxicants and rehabilitation and much more. All designed to influence and motivate fathers, brothers, husbands and sons towards an ideal Islamic lifestyle. A lifestyle referred to by our Creator, Allāh ﷻ in the Holy Qur'ān as the means to salvation and ultimate success.

UK RRP: £5.00

Heroes of Islām

"In the narratives there is certainly a lesson for people of intelligence (understanding)." (12:111)

A fine blend of Islamic personalities who have been recognised for leaving a lasting mark in the hearts and minds of people.

A distinguishing feature of this book is that the author has selected not only some of the most world and historically famous renowned scholars but also these lesser known and a few who have simply left behind a valuable piece of advice to their nearest and dearest. **UK RRP: £5.00**

Ask a Mufti (3 volumes)

Muslims in every generation have confronted different kinds of challenges. Inspite of that, Islām produced such luminary Ulamā who confronted and responded to the challenges of their time to guide the Ummah to the straight path. "Ask A Mufti" is a comprehensive three volume fatwa book, based on the Hanafi School, covering a wide range of topics related to every aspect of human life such as belief, ritual worship, life after death and contemporary legal topics related to purity, commercial transaction, marriage, divorce, food, cosmetic, laws pertaining to women, Islamic medical ethics and much more.

UK RRP: £30.00

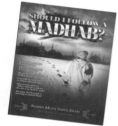

Should I Follow a Madhab?

Taqleed or following one of the four legal schools is not a new phenomenon. Historically, scholars of great calibre and luminaries, each one being a specialist in his own right, were known to have adhered to one of the four legal schools. It is only in the previous century that a minority group emerged advocating a severe ban on following one of the four major schools.

This book endeavours to address the topic of Taqleed and elucidates its importance and necessity in this day and age. It will also, by the Divine Will of Allāh ﷻ dispel some of the confusion surrounding this topic. **UK RRP: £5.00**

Advice for the Students of Knowledge

Allāh ﷻ describes divine knowledge in the Holy Qur'ān as a 'Light'. Amongst the qualities of light are purity and guidance. The Holy Prophet ﷺ has clearly explained this concept in many blessed Ahādeeth and has also taught us many supplications in which we ask for beneficial knowledge.

This book is a golden tool for every sincere student of knowledge wishing to mould his/her character and engrain those correct qualities in order to be worthy of receiving the great gift of Ilm from Allāh ﷻ. **UK RRP: £3.00**

Stories for Children

"Stories for Children" - is a wonderful gift presented to the readers personally by the author himself, especially with the young children in mind. The stories are based on moral and ethical values, which the reader will enjoy sharing with their peers, friends, families and loved ones. The aim is to present to the children stories and incidents which contain moral lessons, in order to reform and correct their lives, according to the Holy Qur'ān and Sunnah.

UK RRP: £5.00

Pearls from My Shaykh

This book contains a collection of pearls and inspirational accounts of the Holy Prophet ﷺ, his noble Companions, pious predecessors and some personal accounts and sayings of our well-known contemporary scholar and spiritual guide, Shaykh Mufti Saiful Islām Sāhib. Each anecdote and narrative of the pious predecessors have been written in the way that was narrated by Mufti Saiful Islām Sāhib in his discourses, drawing the specific lessons he intended from telling the story. The accounts from the life of the Shaykh has been compiled by a particular student based on their own experience and personal observation. **UK RRP: £5.00**

Paradise & Hell

This book is a collection of detailed explanation of Paradise and Hell including the state and conditions of its inhabitants. All the details have been taken from various reliable sources. The purpose of its compilation is for the reader to contemplate and appreciate the innumerable favours, rewards, comfort and unlimited luxuries of Paradise and at the same time take heed from the punishment of Hell. Shaykh Mufti Saiful Islām Sāhib has presented this book in a unique format by including the Tafseer and virtues of Sūrah Ar-Rahmān. **UK RRP: £5.00**

Prayers for Forgiveness

Prayers for Forgiveness' is a short compilation of Du'ās in Arabic with English translation and transliteration. This book can be studied after 'Du'ā for Beginners' or as a separate book. It includes twenty more Du'ās which have not been mentioned in the previous Du'ā book. It also includes a section of Du'ās from the Holy Qur'ān and a section from the Ahādeeth. The book concludes with a section mentioning the Ninety-Nine Names of Allāh ﷻ with its translation and transliteration. **UK RRP: £3.00**

Scattered Pearls

This book is a collection of scattered pearls taken from books, magazines, emails and WhatsApp messages. These pearls will hopefully increase our knowledge, wisdom and make us realise the purpose of life. In this book, Mufti Sāhib has included messages sent to him from scholars, friends and colleagues which will be beneficial and interesting for our readers Inshā-Allāh. **UK RRP: £4.00**

Poems of Wisdom

This book is a collection of poems from those who contributed to the Al-Mumin Magazine in the poems section. The Hadeeth mentions "Indeed some form of poems are full of wisdom." The themes of each poem vary between wittiness, thought provocation, moral lessons, emotional to name but a few. The readers will benefit from this immensely and make them ponder over the outlook of life in general.

UK RRP: £4.00

Horrors of Judgement Day
This book is a detailed and informative commentary of the first three Sūrahs of the last Juz namely; Sūrah Naba, Sūrah Nāzi'āt and Sūrah Abasa. These Sūrahs vividly depict the horrific events and scenes of the Great Day in order to warn mankind the end of this world. These Sūrahs are an essential reminder for us all to instil the fear and concern of the Day of Judgement and to detach ourselves from the worldly pleasures. Reading this book allows us to attain the true realization of this world and provides essential advices of how to gain eternal salvation in the Hereafter.

RRP: £5:00

Spiritual Heart
It is necessary that Muslims always strive to better themselves at all times and to free themselves from the destructive maladies. This book focusses on three main spiritual maladies; pride, anger and evil gazes. It explains its root causes and offers some spiritual cures. Many examples from the lives of the pious predecessors are used for inspiration and encouragement for controlling the above three maladies. It is hoped that the purification process of the heart becomes easy once the underlying roots of the above maladies are clearly understood.   **UK RRP: £5:00**

Hajj & Umrah for Beginners
This book is a step by step guide on Hajj and Umrah for absolute beginners. Many other additional important rulings (Masāil) have been included that will Insha-Allāh prove very useful for our readers. The book also includes some etiquettes of visiting (Ziyārat) of the Holy Prophet's 鷺 blessed Masjid and his Holy Grave.

UK RRP £3:00

Advice for the Spiritual Travellers
This book contains essential guidelines for a spiritual Murīd to gain some familiarity of the science of Tasawwuf. It explains the meaning and aims of Tasawwuf, some understanding around the concept of the soul, and general guidelines for a spiritual Murīd. This is highly recommended book and it is hoped that it gains wider readership among those Murīds who are basically new to the science of Tasawwuf.

UK RRP £3:00

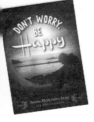

Don't Worry Be Happy
This book is a compilation of sayings and earnest pieces of advice that have been gathered directly from my respected teacher Shaykh Mufti Saiful Islām Sāhib. The book consists of many valuable enlightenments including how to deal with challenges of life, promoting unity, practicing good manners, being optimistic and many other valuable advices. Our respected Shaykh has gathered this Naseehah from meditating, contemplating, analysing and searching for the gems within Qur'anic verses, Ahādeeth and teachings of our Pious Predecessors. **UK RRP £1:00**

Kanzul Bāri

Kanzul Bāri provides a detailed commentary of the Ahādeeth contained in Saheeh al-Bukhāri. The commentary includes Imām Bukhāri's ﷺ biography, the status of his book, spiritual advice, inspirational accounts along with academic discussions related to Fiqh, its application and differences of opinion. Moreover, it answers objections arising in one's mind about certain Ahādeeth. Inquisitive students of Hadeeth will find this commentary a very useful reference book in the final year of their Ālim course for gaining a deeper understanding of the science of Hadeeth. **UK RRP: £15.00**

How to Become a Friend of Allāh ﷺ

The friends of Allāh ﷺ have been described in detail in the Holy Qur'ān and Āhadeeth. This book endeavours its readers to help create a bond with Allāh ﷺ in attaining His friendship as He is the sole Creator of all material and immaterial things. It is only through Allāh's ﷺ friendship, an individual will achieve happiness in this life and the Hereafter, hence eliminate worries, sadness, depression, anxiety and misery of this world. **UK RRP:**

Gems & Jewels

This book contains a selection of articles which have been gathered for the benefit of the readers covering a variety of topics on various aspects of daily life. It offers precious advice and anecdotes that contain moral lessons. The advice captivates its readers and will extend the narrowness of their thoughts to deep reflection, wisdom and appreciation of the purpose of our existence. **UK RRP: £4.00**

End of Time

This book is a comprehensive explanation of the three Sūrahs of Juzz Amma; Sūrah Takweer, Sūrah Infitār and Sūrah Mutaffifeen. This book is a continuation from the previous book of the same author, 'Horrors of Judgement Day'. The three Sūrahs vividly sketch out the scene of the Day of Judgement and describe the state of both the inmates of Jannah and Jahannam. Mufti Saiful Islām Sāhib provides an easy but comprehensive commentary of the three Sūrahs facilitating its understanding for the readers whilst capturing the horrific scene of the ending of the world and the conditions of mankind on that horrific Day. **UK RRP: £5.00**

Andalus (modern day Spain), the long lost history, was once a country that produced many great calibre of Muslim scholars comprising of Mufassirūn, Muhaddithūn, Fuqahā, judges, scientists, philosophers, surgeons, to name but a few. The Muslims conquered Andalus in 711 AD and ruled over it for eight-hundred years. This was known as the era of Muslim glory. Many non-Muslim Europeans during that time travelled to Spain to study under Muslim scholars. The remanences of the Muslim rule in Spain are manifested through their universities, magnificent palaces and Masājid carved with Arabic writings, standing even until today. In this book, Shaykh Mufti Saiful Islām shares some of his valuable experiences he witnessed during his journey to Spain. **UK RRP: £3.00**

Ideal Youth

This book contains articles gathered from various social media avenues; magazines, emails, WhatsApp and telegram messages that provide useful tips of advice for those who have the zeal to learn and consider changing their negative habits and behavior and become better Muslims to set a positive trend for the next generation. **UK RRP:£4:00**

Ideal Teacher

This book contains abundance of precious advices for the Ulamā who are in the teaching profession. It serves to present Islamic ethical principles of teaching and to remind every teacher of their moral duties towards their students. This book will Inshā-Allāh prove to be beneficial for newly graduates and scholars wanting to utilize their knowledge through teaching. **UK RRP:£4:00**

Ideal Student

This book is a guide for all students of knowledge in achieving the excellent qualities of becoming an ideal student. It contains precious advices, anecdotes of our pious predecessors and tips in developing good morals as a student. Good morals is vital for seeking knowledge. A must for all students if they want to develop their Islamic Knowledge. **UK RRP:£4:00**

Ideal Parents

This book contains a wealth of knowledge in achieving the qualities of becoming ideal parents. It contains precious advices, anecdotes of our pious predecessors and tips in developing good parenthood skills. Good morals is vital for seeking knowledge. A must for all parents . **UK RRP:£4:00**

Ideal Couple

This book is a compilation of inspiring stories and articles containing useful tips and life skills for every couple. Marriage life is a big responsibility and success in marriage is only possible if the couple know what it means to be an ideal couple. **UK RRP:£4:00**

Ideal Role Model

This book is a compilation of sayings and accounts of our pious predecessors. The purpose of this book is so we can learn from our pious predecessors the purpose of this life and how to attain closer to the Creator. Those people who inspires us attaining closeness to our Creator are our true role models. A must everyone to read. **UK RRP:£4:00**

Bangladesh– A Land of Natural Beauty

This book is a compilation of our respected Shaykh's journeys to Bangladesh including visits to famous Madāris and Masājid around the country. The Shaykh shares some of his thought provoking experiences and his personal visits with great scholars in Bangladesh. **UK RRP: £4.00**

Pearls from the Quran

This series begins with the small Sūrahs from 30th Juzz initially, unravelling its heavenly gems, precious advices and anecdotes worthy of personal reflection. It will most definitely benefit both those new to as well as advanced students of the science of Tafsīr. The purpose is to make it easily accessible for the general public in understanding the meaning of the Holy Qur'ān. **UK RRP: £10.00**